Hello, Family Members,

Learning to read is one of the most important accomplishments of early childhood. **Hello Reader!** books are designed to help children become skilled readers who like to read. Beginning readers learn to read by remembering frequently used words like "the," "is," and "and"; by using phonics skills to decode new words; and by interpreting picture and text clues. These books provide both the stories children enjoy and the structure they need to read fluently and independently. Here are suggestions for helping your child *before*, *during*, and *after* reading:

Before

- Look at the cover and pictures and have your child predict what the story is about.
- Read the story to your child.
- Encourage your child to chime in with familiar words and phrases.
- Echo read with your child by reading a line first and having your child read it after you do.

During

- Have your child think about a word he or she does not recognize right away. Provide hints such as "Let's see if we know the sounds" and "Have we read other words like this one?"
- Encourage your child to use phonics skills to sound out new words.
- Provide the word for your child when more assistance is needed so that he or she does not struggle and the experience of reading with you is a positive one.
- Encourage your child to have fun by reading with a lot of expression . . . like an actor!

After

- Have your child keep lists of interesting and favorite words.
- Encourage your child to read the books over and over again. Have him or her read to brothers, sisters, grandparents, and even teddy bears. Repeated readings develop confidence in young readers.
- Talk about the stories. Ask and answer questions. Share ideas about the funniest and most interesting characters and events in the stories.

I do hope that you and your child enjoy this book.

—Francie Alexander
Reading Specialist,
Scholastic's Instructional Publishing Group

To Jeff, Matt, Matt, and Brian,
who never believed I was a Shadowette!
—G.S.

For Holland, Jay, and Debbie Gallagher
—J.H.

Library of Congress Cataloging-in-Publication Data
Shaw, Gina.
    Shadows everywhere / by Gina Shaw; illustrated by Joan Holub.
        p.   cm. — (Hello reader! Science. Level 2)
    Summary: Discusses what causes shadows, how they change depending on placement of the light source, and ways to have fun making shadows.
        ISBN 0-590-52296-5
        1. Shades and shadows—Juvenile literature.   [1. Shadows.]
    I. Holub, Joan, ill.   II. Title.   III. Series.
    QC381.6.S52   1999
    535'.4—dc21   98-22213
                                                                        CIP
                                                                        AC

10 9 8 7 6 5 4 3   9/9 0/0 01 02 03

Printed in the U.S.A.   24
First printing, January 1999

Shadows Everywhere

by Gina Shaw
Illustrated by Joan Holub

Hello Reader! Science — Level 2

SCHOLASTIC INC.
Cartwheel ·B·O·O·K·S·®
New York Toronto London Auckland Sydney

It's a bright day.
The sun is shining
in front of you.
You walk.
Something follows you.

You run.
It runs.

You stop.
It stops.

You hop on one foot.
It hops on the
same foot!

You look behind you.
What do you see?
You see your shadow.

Everything can have a shadow.

A big wheel and small
balloons do.
Cotton candy and all
baseballs, too.
Buildings and fences
and flowers and benches —
to name a few!

Shadows are everywhere.

Here's how a shadow is made.

A bright light shines
on an object.
The object blocks the light.
A dark area forms
behind the object.
This darkness is the shadow.

You can make shadows.
Point a flashlight at a wall.
Be sure the room is dark.

Hold your hand in front
of the flashlight.
Look at the wall.
Do you see the shadow
of your hand on the wall?

You can make shadows
with other objects, too.
Try a ruler, a book, or a toy.
Use a fork, a ball,
or a pencil.

Try making shadows
large or small.
Shine a flashlight
on the wall.
Hold a toy close
to the flashlight.

Look at the shadow.
It is large.
That's because the toy
is blocking out a lot of light.

Now, hold the toy away
from the flashlight.

The shadow on the wall
is smaller.
That's because the toy
isn't blocking out much light.

Hold the toy in front of the
flashlight in different places.

Are the shadows big?
Can you make them small?

Shadows can also change
sizes outdoors.
In the morning and afternoon,
the sun is low in the sky.

The buildings are blocking
out a lot of light.
Their shadows are tall.

In the middle of the day, the sun
is directly above the buildings.
Now, the buildings block out
less light.
Their shadows are short.

When you stand in the building's shade, you are in its shadow!

Did you know that night
is a shadow?
Here's why:

The sun shines on one side
of Earth.
When this side of Earth faces
the sun, we have day.

The other side of Earth
is in shadow.

This shadow makes the night.

When our part of Earth
is in shadow, we have night.

You can have lots of fun
with shadows.
Shine a light on a wall.
Be sure the room is dark.
Hold your hands between
the light and the wall.

Try making a bird, a duck, a wolf, and a goat.

bird

duck

wolf

goat

Move your hands to make
the pictures move.

rabbit

Do you remember how to make
shadow pictures large and small?

Here are some more shadows
for you to try — a rabbit,
a turkey, an eagle,
a dog, and a butterfly.

turkey

eagle

dog

butterfly

Can you make other things?

Put on a shadow play
for your family or neighbors.
Make up stories.
Practice with a friend.
Have fun!

Shadow Play by Matt and Em